WHAT A TIME TO JOURNAL

WORK OUT WHY YOU ARE ALREADY ENOUGH

CHIDERA EGGERUE

Publishing Director Sarah Lavelle
Editor Susannah Otter
Designer Claire Rochford and Alicia House
Head of Production Stephen Lang
Production Controller Katie Jarvis

Published in 2020 by Quadrille, an imprint
of Hardie Grant Publishing

Quadrille
52–54 Southwark Street
London SE1 1UN
quadrille.com

Cataloguing in Publication Data: a catalogue record
for this book is available from the British Library.

text © Chidera Eggerue 2018
design © Quadrille 2020

ISBN 9781787135710

Printed in China

YOU.
YOU.
YOU.
YOU.
YOU.

YOU
ARE
SUPPOSED
TO BE
HERE.

SAVE SOME LOVE FOR YOURSELF.

YOU DESERVE IT.

WRITE DOWN 3 REASONS WHY.

'Muddy water is best cleared by leaving it alone.'

Write down your thoughts and set them free:

Now, let it pass:
clarity will arrive when you're ready.

DON'T FOCUS ON TRYING TO BE 'THE BEST'.

FOCUS ON BEING

IRREPLACEABLE.

ONYE SỊ A CHA YA ỊSHỊ A CHARA JOHN: Ọ KWAKWARA ỊSHỊ JOHN KWARA?

translation

he who is asking for the same haircut as John: does he have the same shaped head as John?

'IT' DOESN'T REALLY GET BETTER.

YOU DO.

REMEMBER: YOU'RE IN CONTROL.

PLAN FOR BETTER. VISUALISE YOUR FUTURE. IMAGINE THAT IN A PARALLEL UNIVERSE, THERE IS A VERSION OF YOU THAT LIVES HAVING CHOSEN YOURSELF. THAT VERSION OF YOU IS OPERATING AT YOUR HIGHEST POTENTIAL BECAUSE YOU DESERVE A LIFE YOU HAVE CHOSEN, NOT SETTLED FOR.

if **love** doesn't teach you, **loss** will.

DO NOT CREATE EXPECTATIONS YOU KNOW YOU CANNOT LIVE UP TO.

QUIT OVER-EXPLAINING.

THE WORLD IS STILL GOING TO JUDGE YOU.

Stop waiting for people to give you permission to believe that you are amazing.

You don't need to change; just rearrange your priorities: more you, less them.

_____

_____

_____

_____

_____

_____

_____

_____

_____

_____

_____

_____

_____

_____

_____

_____

_____

_____

_____

NGWERE SHỊ
NA ELU ORJỊ
DA SỊ NA YA GA
ETO ONWEYE
MA ỌWỤRỤ NA
ONWEHỤ ONYE
TORO YA.

translation
the lizard that fell from
an iroko tree said that it
will praise itself if nobody
else does.

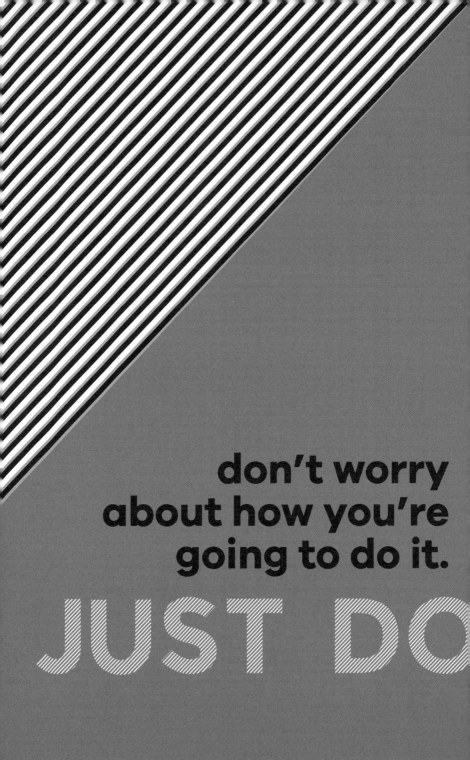

don't worry
about how you're
going to do it.
JUST DO

IT FIRST.

It will all make sense later.

ONYE AKWỌ NA AZU AMAHU NA IJE NA ARA AHỤ.

translation

the person being piggybacked doesn't know how hard the journey is.

For all the times they didn't understand why it was a big deal.

For all the times they tried to talk you out of choosing your joy.

For all the times you almost believed them.

For all the times you celebrated in silence.

For all the times I _____

_____

For all the times I _____

_____

DON'T LET YOUR KINDNESS KILL YOU.

_____

_____

_____

_____

_____

_____

_____

_____

_____

_____

_____

_____

NTỊ CANỤ IWÉ AGAHỤ EWE OBI.

translation
if the ear doesn't hear,
the heart will not be
upset.

THE SOONER
WE STOP
PRETENDING
TO BE
IMMUNE TO
FEELINGS
THAT SCARE
US, THE
SOONER LIFE
WILL BEGIN
TO MAKE
SENSE.

My therapist told me that as long as it is hurting, it is worth acknowledging. Because hurt still hurts even when we try to ignore it.

Write that stuff down!

remember: never feel defeated by a 'no'.

take it as a

'NOT'

LEARN TO 'TAKE ANY LOSS LIKE A BOSS'.

I like to think of mistakes and bad experiences as data I can add to a log which my subconscious refers to when I'm operating from an intuitive place. The more experience you have in the many ways things don't work, the more refined your approach, thinking and gut become. You're always one decision away from a completely different life.

We only learn when we are wrong. What new knowledge have you recently won from your wrongs?

Everything happening to you, is for you.
Life is one big cosmic mess but everything you're going through is pushing you closer to the person you need to be.

Tasting your own magic

Be nice to yourself. Go to Nando's alone. Take walks along the river on your own. Have super-long baths and blast your favourite playlist whilst you do so. Stop waiting for someone to give you that unconditional fairytale love and give it to yourself. Start right now. Unfollow people who give you weird energy. Mute and block people who make you feel uncomfortable for whatever reason. Protect your space and pay no mind to how people may perceive you doing this. You deserve greatness, so give it to yourself. We need to learn to stop feeling so guilty for being kind to ourselves. If you sit around waiting for someone to come and rescue you from yourself, life will pass you by – it ain't gon' happen.

MAMỊ RỊ
ARAHỤ ÁHỤ
MANA
OKỤKỌ
AGÁHỤ
ANYULI YE.

translation

to pee is not hard but a chicken can never do it.

Repeat after me:

I do not owe anybody 'pretty'. Whichever state I choose to show up in will always be enough.
I do not owe anybody 'pretty'. Whichever state I choose to show up in will always be enough.
I do not owe anybody 'pretty'. Whichever state I choose to show up in will always be enough.
I do not owe anybody 'pretty'. Whichever state I choose to show up in will always be enough.
I do not owe anybody 'pretty'. Whichever state I choose to show up in will always be enough.

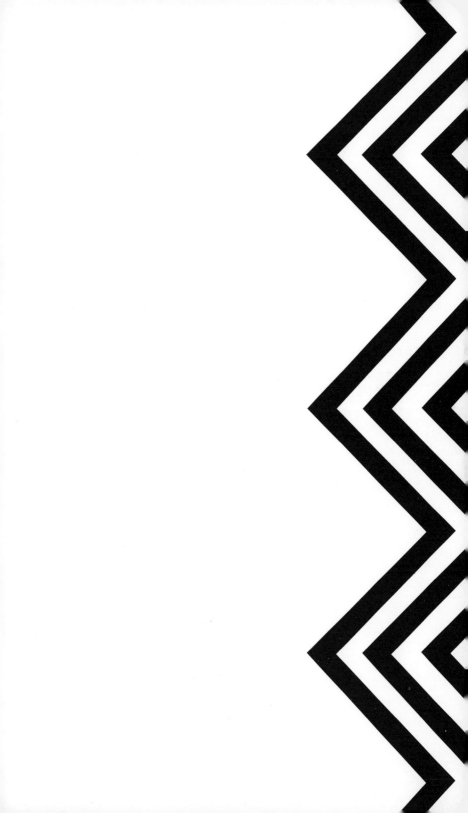

REMEMBER

You are not here for anybody's consumption or amusement.

Sketch out your own space.

What does your happy place look like?

Where do you love to go when you daydream?

Where would you like to take your inner child?

Let it look as abstract and nebulous as the thought itself.

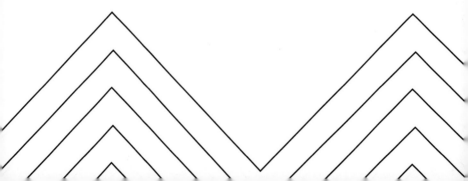

DO YOU KNOW HOW SHORT LIFE IS?

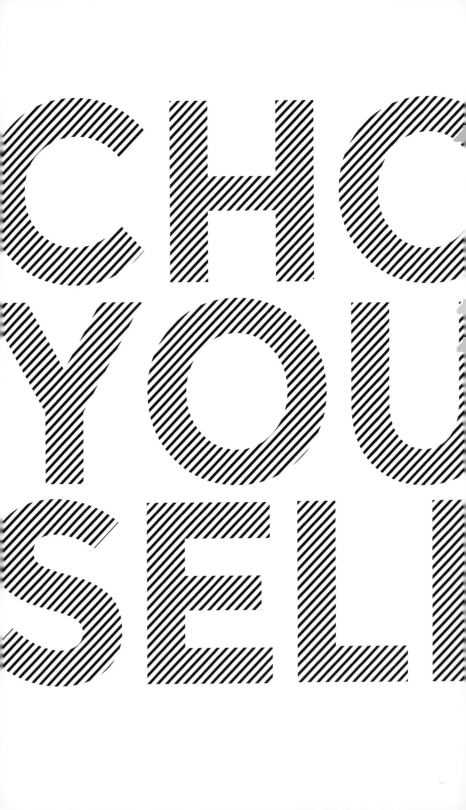

The universe is 13.8 billion years old.

One day on Venus is equal to 243 Earth days.

Whatever it is, it's not worth you losing yourself.

SELF-LOVE IS
THE
LEAST
AGGRESSIVE,
MOST
EFFECTIVE,
FORM OF
INTIMIDATION.
DRAW
YOURSELF
SOME LOVE.

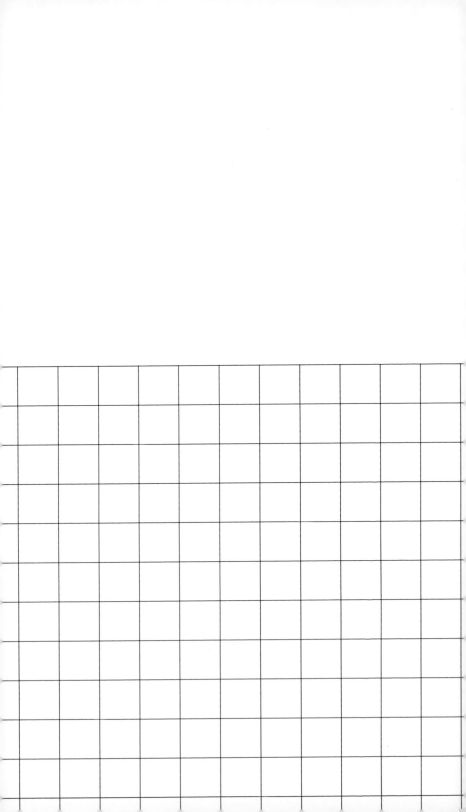

The fear of coming across as 'mean' when asserting our boundaries will keep us in a cycle of being trodden on by people who don't worry about coming across as mean when treating us with a lack of care.

Keeping yourself small is the same as setting yourself on fire to keep others warm. In what ways will you overcome the fear of standing tall in your standards?

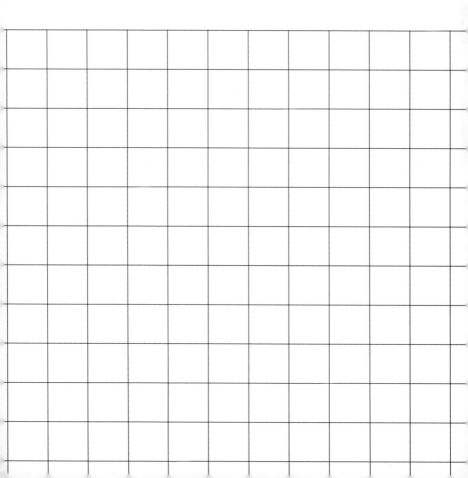

them.
them.
them.
them.
them.

NO MATTER
WHAT,
ALWAYS
REMEMBER:
YOU ARE
ALLOWED
TO CHANGE
YOUR MIND
ABOUT HOW
YOU FEEL
ABOUT OTHER
PEOPLE.

OKE SORO NGWERE NA NMIRI, ỌKỌ NGWERE ỌNAHỤ AKỌ ỌKE.

translation
when the rat follows the lizard out into the rain, it's only the rat that gets soaked.

Stay away
from people
who bring out
the spiteful side
in you.

ONYE JI IHIE NWATA WELIE AKAYA ELU, AKA RAWA YA AHỤ, ỌGA EWEDA YA.

translation
the person holding
a child's toy up high
will eventually put
their arm down when
it starts hurting.

Never give people a **second chance** to **violate** you ... no matter how **small-** or **large-scale** it was.

Write it out of your hair!

WHAT NICE THINGS DO YOU WISH MORE PEOPLE KNEW ABOUT YOU?

Your happiness will always be a trigger to someone. What do you wish you could tell your inner child about the incredible person they are going to grow up to be?

_____

_____

_____

_____

_____

_____

_____

_____

_____

_____

_____

_____

_____

Try to ignore the voice that talks you out of the nice thoughts;

t's the voice of the person who tried to take away your light as a child.

ONYE NA ERE IGBE ỌZỤ NA EKPE EKPERE ỌNWỤ NDE NMADỤ, MANA ỌNA-ATỤ ỤJỌ ỌNWỤ KARỊA ỌNYE ỌBỤLA.

(Horrible people, surprisingly, don't like it when you're horrible to them.)

translation
a coffin merchant prays
for the death of others
but fears death more
than anyone else.

SOMETIMES, 'I FORGOT' ACTUALLY MEANS 'I DIDN'T CARE ENOUGH TO PAY ATTENTION'.

Let's be real: this is subjective. But you'll know when someone you care about forgets something seemingly unforgettable. You'll know when someone you care about overlooks the significant details about you. You'll know when someone prefers the idea of you to the reality of you.

You'll know.

Take the page opposite and really pay attention to how you are feeling, right now.

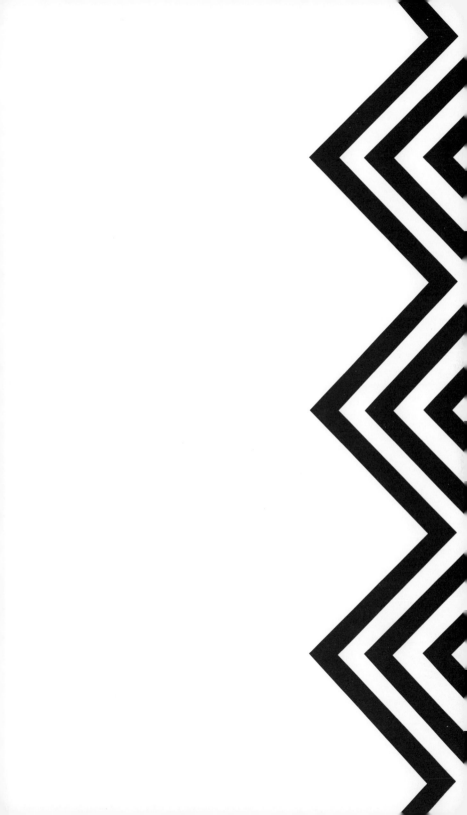

IF YOU FEEL A WEIRD BIT OF GUILT/ DISCOMFORT AFTER SHARING GOOD NEWS,

YOU'RE SHARING YOURSELF WITH THE WRONG PERSON.

ONYE JI IHIE GỊ SORO GỊ NÁ ACHỌ YA, Ị GAHỤ AHỤ YA.

translation
if someone is helping you look for what they stole from you, you'll never find it.

DON'T BE SCARED TO RAISE YOUR

STANDARDS

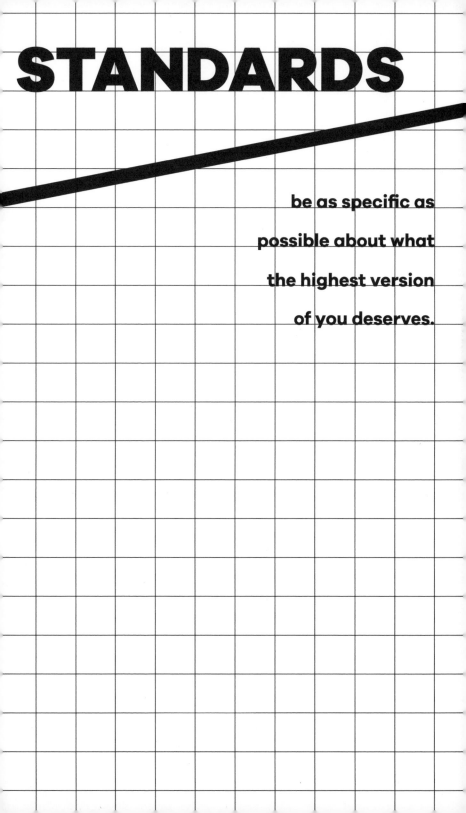

be as specific as
possible about what
the highest version
of you deserves.

NOT EVERY APOLOGY IS GENUINE.

Sometimes, people apologise out of fear.
Sometimes, people apologise because it's convenient.
Sometimes, people apologise without saying 'I'm sorry'
and it feels weird because there's nothing more sincere
than hearing a person say 'I am sorry.'
Sometimes, people apologise to silence you.
Sometimes, people apologise to ask you for something.

**You'll always be able to recognise when it's real.
In the end, it's okay if deep down you still don't
accept the apology. Validate your gut.**

NGE NWATA
NA EBE AKWA
NA-ATỤ AKA,
IHIE NA EMEYA
AKWA NỌ
NGAHỤ.

translation
where a child is crying
and pointing their finger,
what is making them cry
is there.

There's always a reason
why someone is the way
that they are.

**YOU CANNOT SAVE
ANYONE.**

ONLY YOURSELF.

AGWA NTỊ-NTỊ GA-NỤ, EBURU ISHI, YANA NTỊ KWỤRỤ.

translation
when you warn the ear, it doesn't listen, but when you cut the head the ear follows.

SURROUND
YOURSELF
WITH PEOPLE
WHO HONOUR
HOW YOU FEEL.
MAKE A LIST
OF YOUR MOST
CHERISHED
FRIENDS.

ATUWA IKPEM ANYA GHERE OGHE, EKETE ṄAWA NTỊ.

translation
when you start talking
about things with holes
in them, the basket
starts listening.

be nice to people for no reason.

Don't forget to congratulate your friends, no matter how well they are doing.

Sometimes knowing that someone is rooting for you is enough.

Give people their **flowers** while they can still smell them.

HOLD ON TO ON TO
THE
FRIENDS
WHO MAKE
THE
EFFORT TO

SAVE

YOUR

BIRTHDAY IN

THEIR

CALENDAR.

Repeat after me:

What's mine won't miss me.
What's mine won't miss me.
What's mine won't miss me.
What's mine won't miss me.
What's mine won't miss me.
What's mine won't miss me.
What's mine won't miss me.
What's mine won't miss me.
What's mine won't miss me.
What's mine won't miss me.
What's mine won't miss me.
What's mine won't miss me.
What's mine won't miss me.
What's mine won't miss me.
What's mine won't miss me.
What's mine won't miss me.
What's mine won't miss me.
What's mine won't miss me.
What's mine won't miss me.
What's mine won't miss me.
What's mine won't miss me.

What's mine won't miss me.

YOU'LL MEAN THE WORLD TO SOMEONE ONE DAY*

*And it won't just be your mum.

us. us.
us. us.
us. us.
us. us.
us. us.

IT'S OKAY TO WANT TO BE LOVED.

Love and
pride are
like oil
and
water.
The two
will
never

mix.

MIXED
SIGNALS

Mixed signals aren't mysterious.

Mixed signals are the prelude to manipulation.

Once you snap out of the fear of being alone,
you become invincible. Your life finally becomes
yours to shape.

Go ahead and sketch it out!

EMPTY PROMISES ARE OFTEN A DISTRACTION. PROMISES ARE OFTEN A DISTRACTION.

Stop hanging out

h people who

- talk over you in group conversations. They do not respect you.

- love to dump their problems on you while making no room to listen to yours.

- change the way they treat you when they're around people they want to suck up to.

- only support you when it benefits them.

- you show up for and support, but when it's your turn they have an excuse ready, every time.

- also hang out with people who don't like you. As much as it's possible to be civil, it's near impossible to remain 'neutral' between enemies.

- only invite you to events to make themselves look good.

- conceal their friendship with you because of what their other friends may think.

- only appear in your life to find out how they can better themselves, then disappear.

- constantly go out of their way to hang out with people they swear they don't like.

Stop hanging out with people who think it's cool to trick other people. Manipulation of people's feelings isn't anything to be proud of.

Stop hanging out with people who keep flaking on you without making the effort to rearrange plans. They don't care about you or your time.

Stop hanging out with people who love to talk you out of your ambitions but hide behind 'playing devil's advocate'.

Stop hanging out with people who make you feel embarrassed about things you are passionate about

Stop hanging out with people who ditch you when you are in a dark and lonely place mentally. They were never your friends to begin with.

Stop hanging out with people who don't know how to be honest with themselves. They will never be honest with you either.

Stop hanging out with people who make jokes out of your insecurities, then, when you feel offended, tell you that you can't 'take a joke'.

Stop hanging out with people who tell you of malicious things said about you behind your back but not what they said in response to them.

Ị TUO ONYE SHIRI IHE, Ọ SHIE ỌDỌ.

translation
when you praise the person who cooked, they will cook again.

EXPLAINING WHY YOU FEEL HURT IS NOT ALWAYS WORTH IT.

But writing it here is.

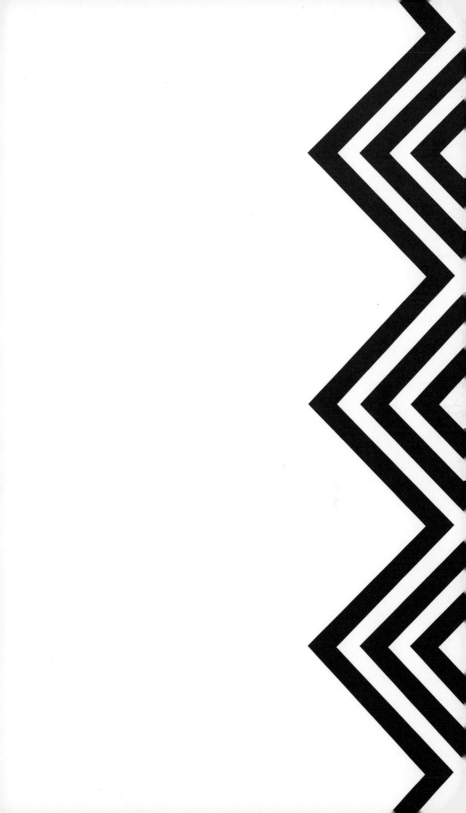

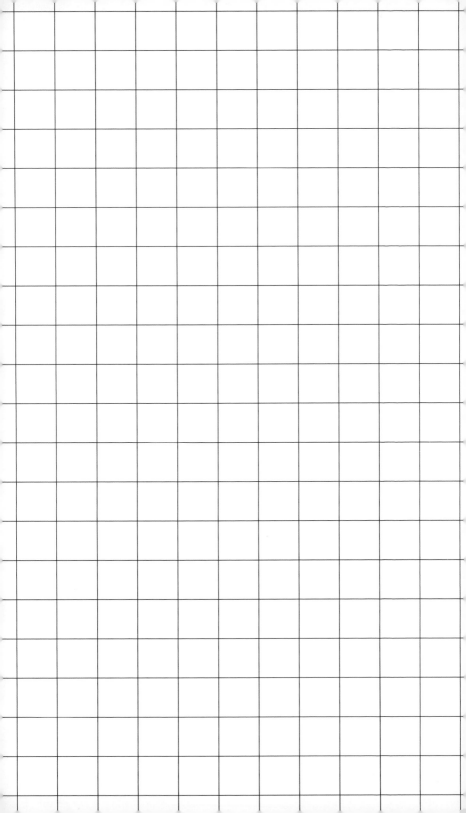

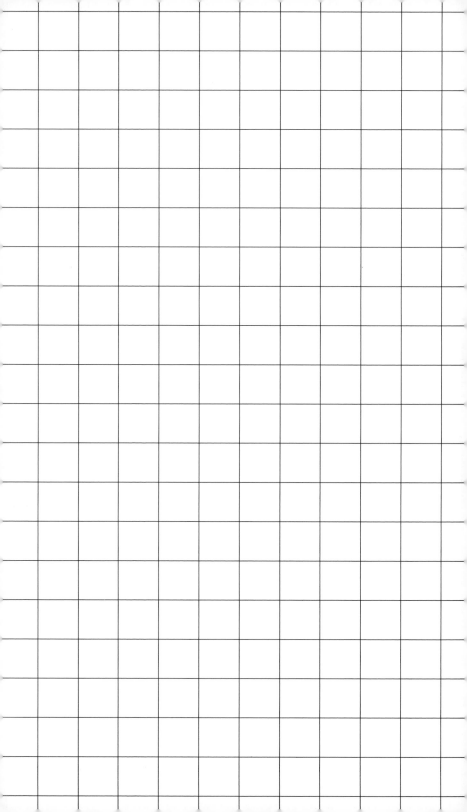

Lower your expectations of others.

Raise your expectations of yourself.

Write your raised expecations here:

NWA SỊ NA
NNEYE AGAHỤ
ARAHA ỤRA,
AGAHỤ ARAHA
KEYE.

translation
the child that says their mother will not sleep, will also not sleep.

NEVER SETTLE FOR LAZY LOVE.

YOU DESERVE BETTER.

Ọ CHOGA MGBALAGA SỊ A RUỌLA YA ANYA.

translation
when someone is looking for an excuse to escape, they'll blame anything.

TRY NOT
TO SHARE
YOURSELF WITH
PEOPLE WHO
DON'T WANT
TO MAKE ROOM
FOR

YOU.

YOU ARE THE
KEY, FEEL FREE
TO LEAVE.

IF IT HURTS A
LOT ALL THE
TIME, IT AIN'T
LOVE, IT'S
PRISON.

EZIGBO ỤKA NA ESHI ŃA UDE NMAYA NA-APỤTA.

translation
out of the wine, comes
the truth.

CERTAIN MISTAKES NEED TO BE MADE, IN ORDER FOR THE

REAL GROWTH

TO BEGIN.

IT IS VERY OKAY TO CHANGE YOUR MIND ABOUT PEOPLE.

ACCEPTED APOLOGIES
ARE NOT CONTRACTS.

REGRET
WORSE
REJECTI

IS /

THAN

ON.

THERE IS NO SHAME IN PAIN

Feel it all and remind yourself that whatever it is that you are feeling right now – be it happiness, sadness or even boredom – it is temporary and will pass like the seasons do. You've got this. Keep your head up, stay strong. It'll get better soon.

IKE ANAHỤ
AGBAGO
AGBAGO,
ỌNA AGBADA
ÁGBADA.

translation
physical strength never
remains permanent. it
must eventually decline.

remember

why

you

left.

FEEL SECURE IN YOUR SOLITUDE

Bestselling author of
What a Time To Be Alone and
Scribble Yourself Feminist,
Chidera Eggerue is an acclaimed,
writer and feminist. Referred to
by *Elle* magazine as a 'millennial
mastermind' Chidera created the
hashtag #SAGGYBOOBSMATTER
and has over 300k followers
across her social media accounts.
She has been featured in *Elle*,
Vogue, *Grazia* and *Stylist*.

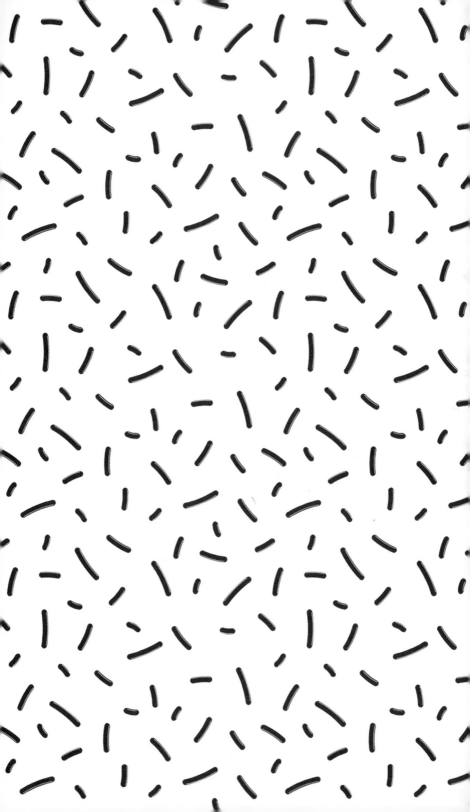

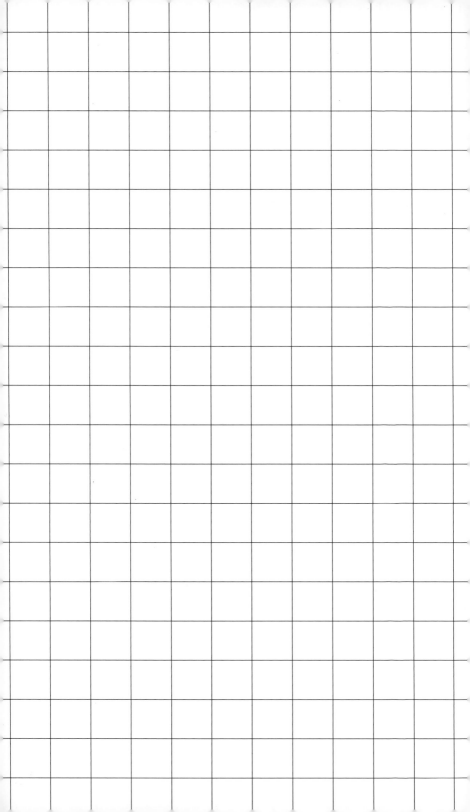